HORRIBLE SCIENCE

ANNUAL 2009

THIS BOOK
BELONGS TO:

_____

_____

SCHOLASTIC

DEAR READER...

Welcome to your
HORRIBLE SCIENCE ANNUAL 2009!
...and what a humongously horrible treat we have in store for you – this year's annual is stuffed full of foul facts and squishy science. We've got raptors, rotting T rexes and robots, blood-sucking bugs, bullet-dodging spies and freaky flying fellows, as well as loads of puzzles and things to do. This is the kind of info your science teachers would NEVER allow you to get your hands on!

CONTENTS

T REX WRECKED!

Sixty-five million years ago, an asteroid had a huge impact on dinosaur-life. Let's peek inside a putrefying corpse of a Tyrannosaurus…

1. The impact (**1a**) made an enormous splash of dust, plunging the world into darkness and cold. With only scales (**1b**) to keep them warm, the dinos chilled out forever (**1c**). Brrr!

2. Eventually the dust settled, leaving a telltale layer of powdery rare metals in the rocks.

3. Gross gases guffing out of volcanoes (**3a**) made the rain turn into acid (**3b**). This did for both the plants and the veggie dinosaurs T rex ate. The gases may also have attacked the ozone layer. Surviving dinos would have got a terrible tan from UV damage (**3c**).

4. Any dinosaurs within thousands of kilometres of the impact would have got a lethal lungful of soot.

5. After the impact the world got colder and then much hotter. The temperature of reptile eggs decides whether they hatch male or female. Warm eggs hatch males. If this was also the case for dinos, no females would mean no eggs = egg-stinction!

6. T rex was marvellously well-adapted for his world. But even with his phenomenally powerful legs (**6a**), he couldn't run away from climate change. (Hear that, humans?). T rex also had a superb sense of smell.

The part of its brain that sensed smell (**6b**) was the size of an orange. (In humans it's the size of a pea.)

7. T rex's teeth were especially adapted for slicing flesh. Being so specialized means that when the world changes, you can't…

8. …unlike the adaptable mini-mammals. These cunning ratty critters made it through the great extinction.

TERRIBLE DIZZY LIZZIES

The heyday of the dinosaurs ('terrible lizards') was a pretty hazardous time. Let's join one clawed critter to discover just how tough it could be…

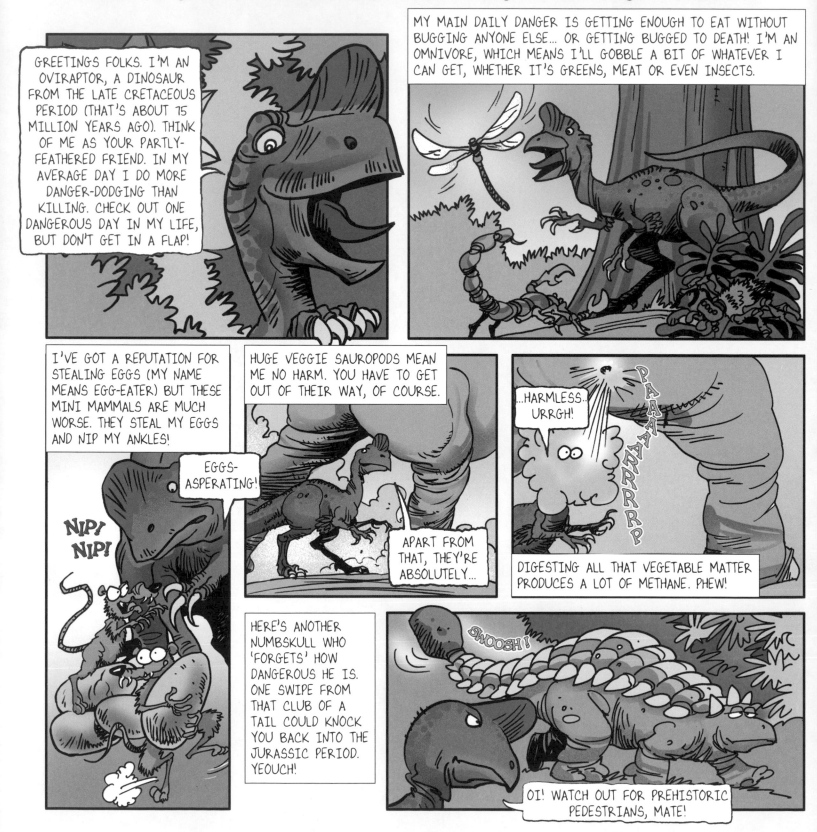

GREETINGS FOLKS. I'M AN OVIRAPTOR, A DINOSAUR FROM THE LATE CRETACEOUS PERIOD (THAT'S ABOUT 75 MILLION YEARS AGO). THINK OF ME AS YOUR PARTLY-FEATHERED FRIEND. IN MY AVERAGE DAY I DO MORE DANGER-DODGING THAN KILLING. CHECK OUT ONE DANGEROUS DAY IN MY LIFE, BUT DON'T GET IN A FLAP!

MY MAIN DAILY DANGER IS GETTING ENOUGH TO EAT WITHOUT BUGGING ANYONE ELSE… OR GETTING BUGGED TO DEATH! I'M AN OMNIVORE, WHICH MEANS I'LL GOBBLE A BIT OF WHATEVER I CAN GET, WHETHER IT'S GREENS, MEAT OR EVEN INSECTS.

I'VE GOT A REPUTATION FOR STEALING EGGS (MY NAME MEANS EGG-EATER) BUT THESE MINI MAMMALS ARE MUCH WORSE. THEY STEAL MY EGGS AND NIP MY ANKLES!

EGGS-ASPERATING!

NIP! NIP!

HUGE VEGGIE SAUROPODS MEAN ME NO HARM. YOU HAVE TO GET OUT OF THEIR WAY, OF COURSE.

APART FROM THAT, THEY'RE ABSOLUTELY…

…HARMLESS… URRGH!

PAAAAARRRRP

DIGESTING ALL THAT VEGETABLE MATTER PRODUCES A LOT OF METHANE. PHEW!

HERE'S ANOTHER NUMBSKULL WHO 'FORGETS' HOW DANGEROUS HE IS. ONE SWIPE FROM THAT CLUB OF A TAIL COULD KNOCK YOU BACK INTO THE JURASSIC PERIOD. YEOUCH!

SWOOSH!

OI! WATCH OUT FOR PREHISTORIC PEDESTRIANS, MATE!

Dino Doomsday

Life and times in the Cretaceous could be bloody and brutal. The daily hunt for dinner involved a lot of ducking swinging spikes and risking getting gobbled. But things were about to get a whole lot worse...

Sixty-five million years ago, something very bad happened in the world. Suddenly the dinosaurs, who had been the top reptiles, died out completely, never to return. It wasn't just the dinosaurs that suffered – three-quarters of all animals on Earth kicked the can. Land animals weighing over 25kg were wiped out.

The best explanation we have for this is that a ginormous asteroid hit Earth. Geologists have found a monster crater made by an asteroid at exactly the  right time (65 million years ago in the sea off the Yucatan peninsula in Mexico). Could this be the one that brought doomsday for the dinos? Any asteroid that made a hole that big would have been 10,000 times more destructive than all the nuclear bombs that have ever been built.

Nuclear winter

The impact would have caused terrible earthquakes, lethal tsunami tidal waves, raging forest fires and, worst of all, a huge mushroom cloud of smoke and dust climbing high in the atmosphere. This dust would have blocked out the Sun, causing a twilight that would have lasted for years.

Without the Sun, the temperature plummeted. The dust caused killer storms and acid rain. Plants withered and died, and without food to eat, plant-eating dinosaurs would have quickly gone the same way. This would have spelled the end for meat-eaters too, with less and less food to chase.

As usual, life is more interesting than theory, and now scientists think the dinos may have been hit with a triple whammy. The Earth was cooling down anyway and the weather was getting unpredictable – dangerous for creatures who aren't very good at keeping warm. At the time there were loads of volcanoes in South Asia, pumping out nasty, noxious chemicals into the atmosphere. Maybe they were even caused by the Yucatan asteroid, the third and final straw for the poor reptiles.

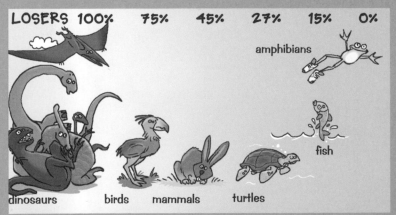

LOSERS 100%   75%   45%   27%   15%   0%

amphibians

fish

dinosaurs   birds   mammals   turtles

Dangerous and Deadly

Some scientists reckon that the Sun is actually part of a two-star system. They think there might be another star orbiting around the Sun. Every time it comes around, it disturbs the asteroids and comets floating out there in the solar system, sending them hurtling towards Earth. Their best guess is to wait another 26 million years to find out. Luckily, none of us will be around to see if their scary predictions are true!

BITS OF A BIGGER PICTURE

Fossils are fab for digging the dirt on extinct species. They give clues to how ancient plants and animals lived and died.

1. Fossils are parts or traces of dead plants or animals that have been turned into stone or other minerals. You sometimes see the shape of a whole creature....

2. ...or much more likely, a small bone fragment, or a leaf or tooth – such as this one from a savage shark that lived about 400 mya.

3. Some fossils, such as this T rex skull, are huge. (This one's even bigger than normal!)

4. Fossil hunting is like treasure seeking. Imagine digging up the stone skull of a 12,000-year-old sabre-toothed cat (**4a**), or splitting a rock to find the print of a nightmarish dragonfly (**4b**)! Like pieces of a jigsaw, if you could find every fossil you'd have a complete picture of life on Earth. The trouble is, nearly all the pieces are missing – only a tiny fraction of the thousands of extinct species have been fossilized!

5. Hard things such as shells and teeth are most likely to be fossilized, especially when buried in the gloopy sludge of ocean beds. That's why tough trilobites and crusty ammonites (**5a**) are plentiful, while fossils of softies, such as worms, aren't.

6. Winged insects are very fragile, but are sometimes found fossilized in amber – tree resin.

7. A few soft-bodied creatures have been found in the sea bed – including Hallucigenia and some of the oldest known fossils – tiny worms from about 600 mya (**7a**)!

8. No doubt many fossils have yet to be found, but even so, most species never were and never will be fossilized. So, if you find jigsaws bone-wearyingly boring, you might want to take a break from fossil hunting!

THE MOUTH OF THIS CAVE LOOKS A BIT ODD...

SHOVE OFF!

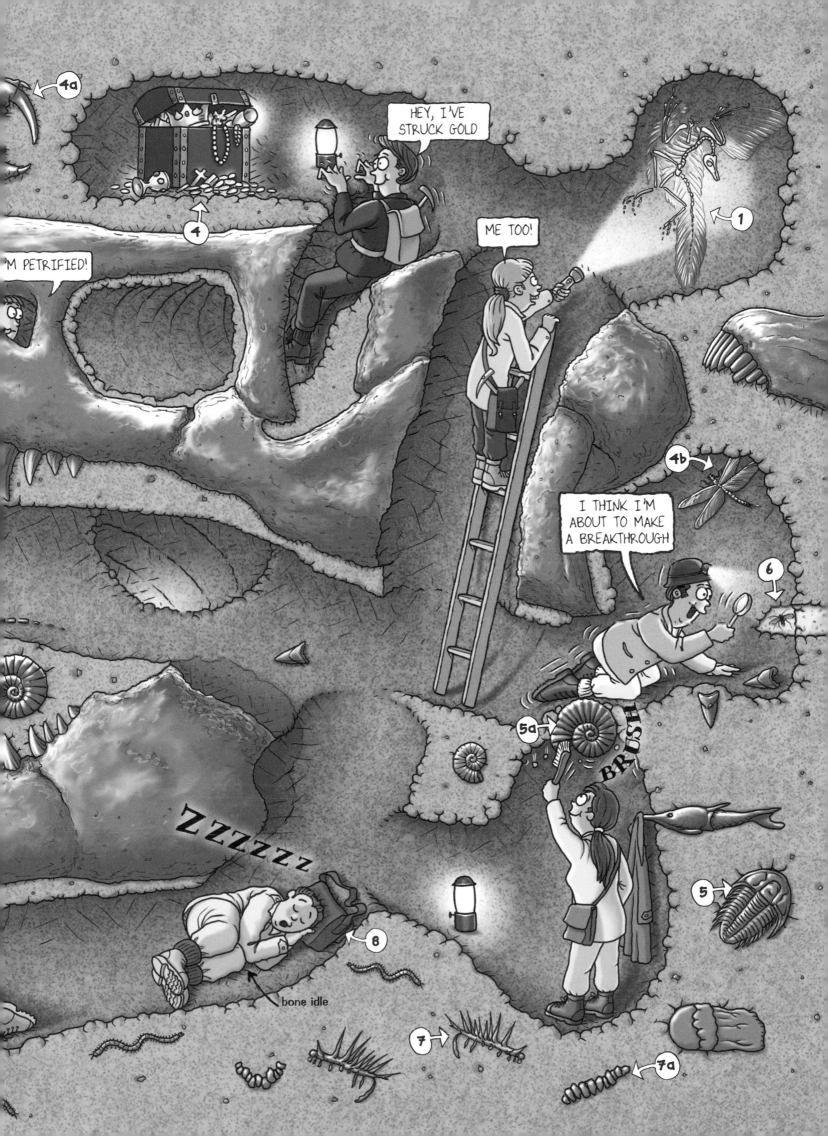

HORRIBLE HUNTERS

It wasn't just the vegetable chompers that went around in herds. Gangs of bloodthirsty predators were also on the prowl in the Cretaceous…

Dinosaurs could live to about 70 years old (and some of the very big ones might have gone on for 130 years), but very few dinos died of old age. Almost all checked out early, with nasty, grisly and violent deaths. If you were a peaceful plant-munching dino, the chances were that the last thing you'd feel was the sharp pain of a raptor's lethal toe-claw as it punched through your scales. The last thing you'd see were its mean, calculating eyes, as its mouth gaped open…

raptors had remarkably big brains for their size – this one is already figuring out how to get YOU!

forward-facing eyes made these killers very good at judging distances – an essential slasher skill!

lethally sharp toe claws

The pint-sized raptors only grew as tall as a human, but they were the ultimate killing machines (this group of reptiles includes the famous velociraptors). Like packs of wild dogs today, they hunted as an organised team, using intelligence, cunning and deadly speed, and they were scarily good at bringing down prey much bigger than themselves. On the other end of the scale was the double-decker-bus-sized T rex. This monster killer weighed seven tonnes when fully grown and scoffed about 2.5kg of meat every day.

DINO FACT FILE

NAME: Deinonychus (dine-on-ee-kus)

NICKNAME: Terrible Claw

FAMILY: Raptors

SIZE: 3–4m long

WHEN: Early Cretaceous

FRIGHTENING FACTS: These guys had a 12cm-long, razor-sharp claw on each toe. Attacking in packs, they leapt at their victims, slashing deep cuts with these claws. The prey would bleed to death.

DEADLY DETAILS: Raptors could move at about 60km/h. Before prey knew what was happening it would all be over.

SORRY – YOU CAN'T HAVE A RIDE

THAT'S OK, WE JUST WANT YOUR HIDE!

DINO FACT FILE

NAME: Tyrannosaurus rex

NICKNAME: T rex

FAMILY: Tyrannosaurs

SIZE: 12–13m long

WHEN: Late Cretaceous

FRIGHTENING FACTS:
A joint halfway along its jaw allowed T rex to open its mouth so wide it could swallow you whole. Its curving, dagger-like teeth could rip though meat, sinew and bone.

DEADLY DETAILS: A phenomenally good sense of smell would have enabled T rex to sniff out any prey or carcasses in the area – dead or alive, it probably wasn't too fussy about which type of meat it got!

BET YOU NEVER KNEW!

Despite its fearsome reputation, there are some baffling facts about T rex. No one is quite sure how it used its tiny arms or why they were so puny – they couldn't even reach its mouth. Maybe they were used to hold prey or to help lift T rex off the ground after resting, but they certainly wouldn't have been any good for playing conkers!

HOLD IT FURTHER OUT!

Oh For a Quiet Life...

With so many terrifying predators around, dinosaurs that weren't equipped with a set of scary teeth came bristling with a whole range of defences.

The fairly harmless stygimoloch (stij-ee-moll-uck) – meaning demon from the River Styx – liked nothing more than munching shrubbery, but to give the impression that it was a fearsome customer it had a frightening array of large horns on its head.

EEK! A MONSTER!

The ankylosaurs (an-kyle-oh-sore) were the armoured vehicles of the prehistoric past. Even though they were mild-mannered vegetarians, they were built like tanks and wore a HUGE club on the end of a muscle-packed tail. Boffins have called this lethal bone-ball a 'thagomizer', after a joke in their favourite cartoon 'The Far Side', and because that's exactly what it would do to you if you got in its way!

CARE TO JOIN THE CLUB?

MAKE FOSSIL CRITTERS

Not all fossil finds are genuine - some devious devils cook up fake ones to fool the boffins and make a quick buck. Here's your chance to create a loony prehistoric relic of your own!

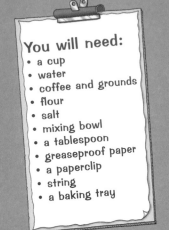

You will need:
- a cup
- water
- coffee and grounds
- flour
- salt
- mixing bowl
- a tablespoon
- greaseproof paper
- a paperclip
- string
- a baking tray

1 Fill a small cup with used coffee grounds from a percolator. Tip the coffee grounds into a mixing bowl. Measure out one cup of flour and add this to the bowl. Then add half a cup of salt. Stir the mixture well.

STIR

2 Make half a cup of black coffee and let it go cold. Then add the cold coffee a little at a time into the mixing bowl, stirring it around until you have a thick, gloopy paste.

SPLURGE!

3 Knead the 'dough' mix and spread large biscuit-like dollops on greaseproof paper. Leave them to set and harden up for a few hours. The mix should turn firm and rubbery and start to look like a piece of brown rock.

SPLAT!

4 Press your thumb into the 'rock' to make the body of a prehistoric pest insect, such as a ghastly beetle.

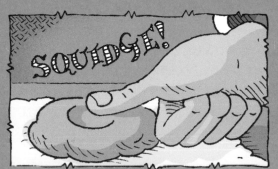
SQUIDGE!

SCRAPE!

5 Using the end of a bent-out paperclip, scrape six legs, carve out a head and add two pointy antennae. Also scratch a few marks around the fossil critter to resemble cracks in the rock. Poke a hole through at the top to thread string through.

7 Who knows, these prehistoric remains may even fool some silly old fossils!

6 Leave the 'rock' to harden fully for a day or so, then tie string through the hole so you can hang it up or hold it without breaking the delicate 'fossils'!

PUZZLES

SPIT IT OUT!

Some of the things volcanoes spit out have got some weird names. Can you guess which of these things are names for stuff that really erupts out of volcanoes and which ones have been made up?

toilet
curtains
hat
grand piano
BOOOM!
pumice stone
rope
bomb
fish
hair
breadcrust
ash
pillow
sandwich

SPOT THE DIFFERENCE

Can you spot the six difference in the pictures below?

Wicked Wordsearch

Take a look and see if you can dig up the 12 dynamic dino words in this grid.

S	R	C	Y	C	K	F	D	P	R	T	S	O
P	U	U	R	C	I	D	O	T	P	I	L	D
O	A	K	K	E	L	O	R	S	S	F	L	I
T	S	E	O	O	T	I	Z	Y	S	N	X	P
A	O	R	G	N	A	A	H	O	W	I	L	L
R	N	A	K	S	A	P	C	Q	S	W	L	O
E	I	K	S	P	O	H	T	E	E	E	C	D
C	D	I	U	L	L	S	Y	E	O	W	M	O
I	C	Z	E	C	I	S	S	A	R	U	J	C
R	M	O	P	A	N	G	A	E	A	U	S	U
T	C	M	P	Y	W	P	I	W	N	I	D	S
S	F	T	Y	R	A	N	N	O	S	A	U	R
Q	C	Y	J	G	I	I	I	B	T	Q	U	Y

Coelophysis   Cretaceous   Dinosaur
Diplodocus   Mesozoic   Fossil
Jurassic   Era   Pangaea
Triassic   Triceratops   Tyrannosaur

HORRIBLE HOUSEMATES

Get the feeling that your home is a little over-crowded? Well that's 'cos it is. And here's why…

1. Steamy bathrooms can house manky mould. It may look like a patch of black spots, but under a microscope it's a forest of living pinheads.

2. Cheese mites love smelly old cheese rind. An Austrian cheese called Altenburger, uses cheese mites to give it a special 'musty' taste. Yuck – these Austrians must–y be crazy!

3. Uh–oh! Looks like weevils have got into the rice. These little devils will eat through any dried grain like rice and cereal in no time at all.

4. Flour mites live in the flour – you could say they survive on flour–power (groan)!

5. This rugger–lover has got visitors – headlice. The lice are hard to spot because they're see–through, but their eggs are the white dots called 'nits'. Lice bites itch like mad. That's 'hit' so nice!

6. Booklice crawl about in the spines of books, grazing on mould growing on the glue that holds the spine together.

7. Blood–sucking fleas are some of the most common critters in their 'cat'–egory (geddit?)!

8. 'Woolly bears' are the young larvae of the carpet beetle. They gobble up your clothes and carpets. Vacuum cleaners are their biggest enemy.

9. Dust mites get everywhere. There are about two million of the critters in every double bed feeding on dead skin and dried dribble in your pillows, duvet and mattress. Their only fear is being gobbled up by the dreaded cannibal mite (**9a**).

10. Woodworm aren't worms at all, but beetle larvae.

FLUSH!

HE'S SO CHEESY, HE'S BEGINNING TO GRATE ON ME!

HE GETS ON MY CURDS

THIS IS MITE-Y FINE CHEESE!

HUH!?

I'M THE LESSER OF TWO WEEVILS!

MEEE-OOOW

INSECT EARTH

We humans like to think we run our planet, but there are plenty of other living creatures out there getting very busy and buzzy. And when it comes to sheer numbers, humans are in a tiny minority…

WELCOME TO EARTH, A PLANET CRAWLING WITH LIFE. SOME OF IT'S WARM-BLOODED, SOME TWO-LEGGED, BUT THAT'S REALLY JUST A FEW. WITH 30 MILLION DIFFERENT SPECIES MAKING 85 PER CENT OF THE POPULATION, IT'S REALLY A WORLD OF…

…INSECTS! AND ON INSECT EARTH IT'S JUST AN ORDINARY DAY.

BUZZ

FLUTTER

WRIGGLE

BUT EVERY NOW AND AGAIN, ACCIDENTS CAN HAPPEN…

STOMP

EEK!

BUT LIFE GOES ON, WITH ALL THE USUAL ACTIVITIES…

HUMPH!

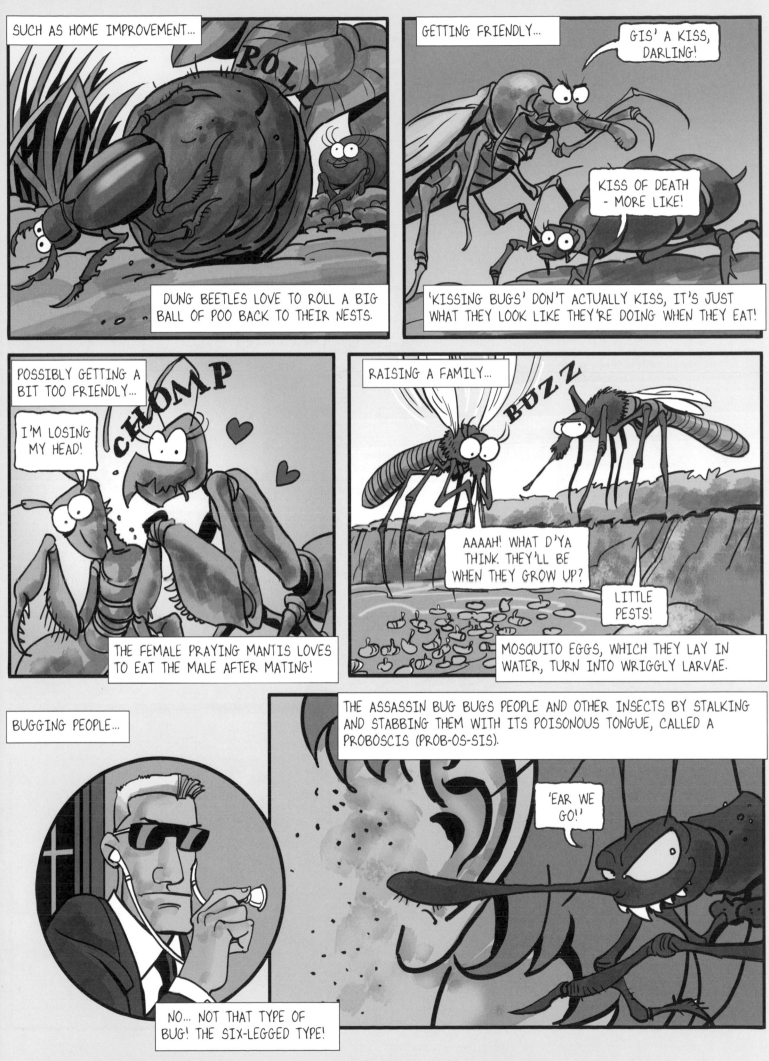

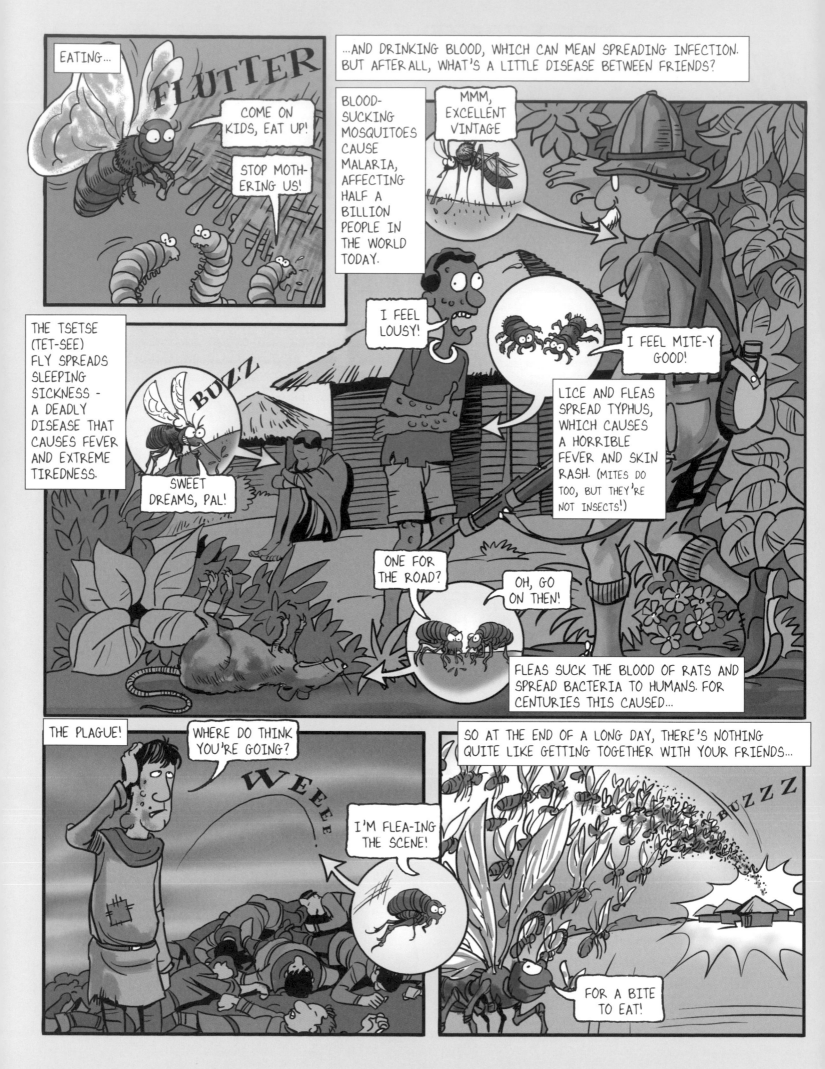

BITING BUGS

The most horrible thing about insects is the way they buzz around and bite us... and suck blood, and sometimes give us vile diseases too.

Bugs are a large group of insects with over 80,000 species. They love slurping veggie juices through their straw-like mouths. Oh yes, and a bit of blood now and then.

STRAWS OUT, LADS!

Flies

There are over 120,000 species of fly. They use one pair of wings for flying (backwards and sideways round your head). They also have the remains of a second pair of wings, like tiny drumsticks, used for balancing. Some like nothing better than to lick the top of a big smelly cowpat… and then pay a visit to your grub!

WIPE YOUR FEET ON THE SANDWICH AND COME IN, KIDS!

Sucking lice

Lice come in about 1000 species. They live on other creatures. It's nice and warm there, and you can always suck a refreshing drop of blood.

Earwigs

Some 1900 species this time! Earwigs get their name from the (wrong) belief that they crawl into your ears with their mean-looking pincers.

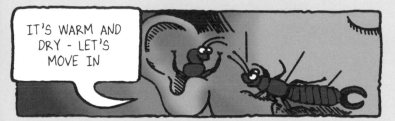

IT'S WARM AND DRY - LET'S MOVE IN

Rogues' Gallery

People often call a crowd of insects a 'plague'. But plagues are really deadly diseases. In the past 10,000 years, more people have died from diseases carried by insects than any other single cause. Help! Check out the chief culprits...

Malarial mosquito

SEX: Female

HABITS: Sucks blood before laying eggs (Mr Mosquito prefers plant juice)

WEAPONS: A long snout for sticking into people and a pump-action saliva gun to stop your blood clotting

LAST SEEN: All over the world. Loiters near water

KNOWN CRIMES: In hot countries, her bite passes on germs that cause malaria. Victims suffer raging fever and feel very hot and then very cold. Responsible for over a million deaths each year.

DANGER RATING: Beware! Two billion people live in areas threatened by the brutal blood-sucker

Tsetse fly

HABITS: Sucks blood. Known to drink up to three times its own weight in a single sitting. Likes a challenge – enjoys biting through rhinoceros skin

LAST SEEN: Many parts of Africa

KNOWN CRIMES: Its bite passes on germs that cause sleeping sickness. This deadly disease causes fever, tiredness and death

DANGER RATING: In Africa, 50 million people are at risk, plus countless cattle, camels, mules, horses, donkeys, pigs, goats, sheep, etc.

LIQUID LUNCH

There's nothing quite like a nice drop of blood for lunch – well, if you're a monstrous mosquito there isn't! Bet you're itching to find out more…

1. The mozzie's mouth is like a straw – perfect for sucking up juicy human blood.

2. These feathery–looking bits act like tiny saws (**2a**) to cut a hole in the skin!

3. To suck up blood the mozzie squirts saliva into the blood vessel. This is what makes a mozzie bite irritatingly itchy! The saliva thins the blood so that it flows easily (**3a**). White blood cells turn up to fight the saliva molecules (**3b**), which is why mozzie bites become swollen.

4. The saliva is made in glands and squirted down though the mouth and into the blood by the saliva pump (**4a**).

5. A powerful sucking muscle pumps the blood from your body, just like a mouth sucking on a straw (**5a**)!

6. It takes about two minutes for a mozzie to suck up a whole bellyful of blood.

7. A mosquito's–eye view of the world.

8. Mozzies don't breathe through the mouth – they breathe through air tubes!

9. Their wings beat 6–8 times a second!

10. Mosquito feet have got tiny claws – great for gripping onto skin.

11. It takes a mozzie 30 seconds to drill into a blood vessel. But it only has three seconds before you feel the bite.

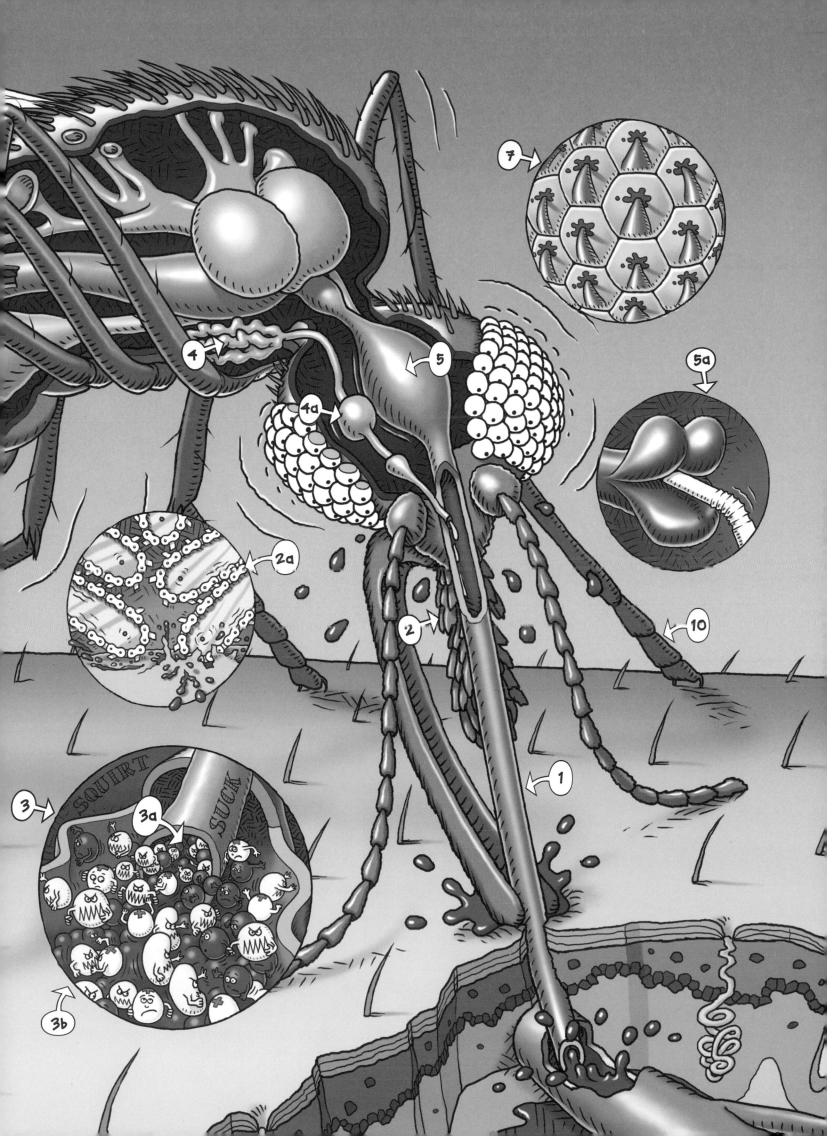

MAKE YOUR OWN BUG CATCHER!

Catching mini monsters in the garden is a tricky business. But with your super bug catcher or 'pooter' you can make inspecting the little critters as easy as breathing!

1 Grab a clean jam jar and ask an adult to make two holes in the lid. The holes should be about the width of a straw.

2 Cut the bottom half of your bendy straws so that they are about 3cm shorter than the height of your jar.

3 Now push a straw through each hole as far as the bendy bit and fill in any gaps with Blu-Tack. Take off the lid and loosely cover the end of one straw with muslin, securing it with the elastic band. Your pooter is ready for some eye-boggling bug action, so head out to the garden or park.

4 ...and suck air up the other straw. Your bug will get sucked through the first straw, and end up in the jar, not your mouth. Phew! That's a relief!

WARNING! When you see this symbol, ask for help from an adult.

26

TINY TERRORS

The first scientist to peer down a microscope tube at pond water came face to face with a scary new world. The residents of this weird and weeny world ain't about to win any beauty contests and they have some really repulsive habits...

The first person to see many of these putrid pipsqueaks was a Dutch scientist called Antony van Leeuwenhoek. One day he went for a stroll alongside the local swampy lake called Berkelse Mere and, for some reason, felt inspired to strip down to his knickerbockers and wade into the green, smelly slop to take a sample of the water.

When he got the soupy sample home he found that it was teeming with tiny terrors. Antony was so excited he wrote letters to the Royal Society, the top science club in Britain.

MICROSCOPIC MONSTERS FACT FILE

NAME: Algae

THE BASIC FACTS: Algae are a type of plant that microscope-mad scientists think are the business! Unlike normal plants, some can swim around under their own steam! They include the green, slimy stuff that you find in ponds.

MONSTROUS DETAILS: Algae thrive in water filled with sewage.

> WANT TO CREATE YOUR OWN ALGAE FARM? DON'T FLUSH YOUR LOO FOR SIX MONTHS!

BET YOU NEVER KNEW!

Protists can breed very fast. For example, a paramecium (pa-ra-me-see-um) divides every 22 hours. In just 66 days it can form a huge slimy ball 1.6km across. A month later it could be as big as the Earth! Luckily, other tiny creatures are public-spirited enough to eat the paramecium before it takes over the world!

WELL, I WISH THE TINY CREATURES WOULD EAT A BIT FASTER!

OOER!

ERK!

ARRGH!

Prowling protists

As well as a whole load of awful algae in his bilge water, Antony also had the first look at protists. Here's what a very famous protist, the amoeba (am-ee-ba) looks like...

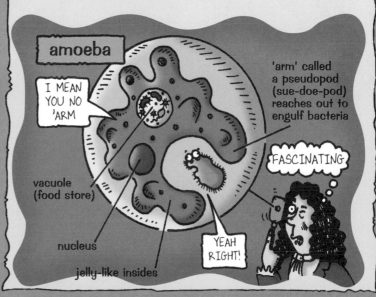

amoeba

I MEAN YOU NO 'ARM

'arm' called a pseudopod (sue-doe-pod) reaches out to engulf bacteria

FASCINATING

vacuole (food store)

nucleus

YEAH RIGHT!

jelly-like insides

DOWN THE PLUGHOLE

When the kitchen drain gets a going over, it's war – chemical war that is, as the grimebusters go head-to-head with the gunk and slime lurking in the darkened depths. Cleaning has never been so dirty!

LET'S GO AND BUG SOMEONE ELSE

RUN AWAY!

BLURB

A Beastly Battle in the U-Bend

1. As this crack team of chemical cleaners is poured down the plughole the action begins. They are fired up to kick bacterial butt.

2. First up for the cleaning crew are the smellies – drifting stinkers who live between the plughole and the U-bend. But they're no match for the grimebusters.

3. The greasies are a tougher nut for the clean-up champs to crack. Fat from fried breakfasts and greasy gunk from gravy dinners builds up and clings to the sides of the drain. But the boys have a two-pronged plan. They get heated when they meet water to melt the grease away (**3a**). Then they convert some of the fat to soap, washing away even more of the messy muck (**3b**).

4. Once they get into the soupy slop, the battle really begins. The heroic heavies square up with the free-floating beastly bacteria. They have another secret weapon up their sleeves – they make bubbles of hydrogen gas that stir up the water.

5. The U-bend water stops insects scuttling in and nauseating niffs wafting back from the sewer, but it also collects a foul layer of gunge. The chemical crew get to work dislodging the gunk (**5a**).

6. Towards the sewer is where the really strange stuff lives. Slime cities built by oozing bacteria grow and eat away at the pipes. But the grimebusters drive the bugs round the (U) bend!

I'M DRILLED TO BE PART OF THIS TEAM

'AIRY MOMENTS!

Welcome to the Super Stunt Airshow for early planes from 1900 to the 1930s! We hope you won't find it too much of a 'drag'. It'll give you a 'lift' and you'll be stunned by the skill and control of these fabulous flyers - well, mostly!

1. The Wright brothers made the first powered flight in 1903 at Kitty Hawk in North Carolina. When it came to weight, lift and drag, the team certainly got it 'Wright'!

2. George Spratt helped the Wright brothers develop planes. In 1909 this rickety 'CarPlane' stayed in the air for a record-breaking two hours.

3. In 1912 Calbraith Rodgers had a nasty accident when birds flew into his plane and he crashed.

4. Another of Cal's planes, Vin Fiz, crossed America but most of the bits of it dropped off on the way! The propellers were turned by bicycle chains.

5. In 1914 American stunt star Lincoln Beachey pitted his speedy motorised plane against a racing car.

6. Clyde Edward 'Upside-Down' Pangborn made crowds gasp with his stunts in the 1920s. Here he tries to get from a car to his plane. Plane stupid!

7. Octave Chanute was a very early pioneer of flight before motors were fitted. His wing designs were great gliders.

8. Louis Blériot crossed the English Channel in 1909. But this tail spin is making him 'Blériot' eyed!

9. The classic Tiger Moth made its first flight on 26 October 1931, and was popular with the RAF, as it was good at tricky manoeuvres. Check out this barrel roll!

10. De Havilland's DH-4 was used by the US Air Service in France during World War I, primarily for observation.

11. With a more powerful engine, the 1930s Stearman was a superb stunt plane and it's doing the loop-the-loop. Yikes, it's lost a pilot! Phew! Well caught, Sir!

12. The Fiesler Storch is a monoplane, with one wing on each side of the fuselage.

FOOLISH FALL GUYS

Next time you're fed up of waiting for your delayed holiday flight, take comfort from the fact that to get from the first kite to a decent glider, man had to wait 3000 years!

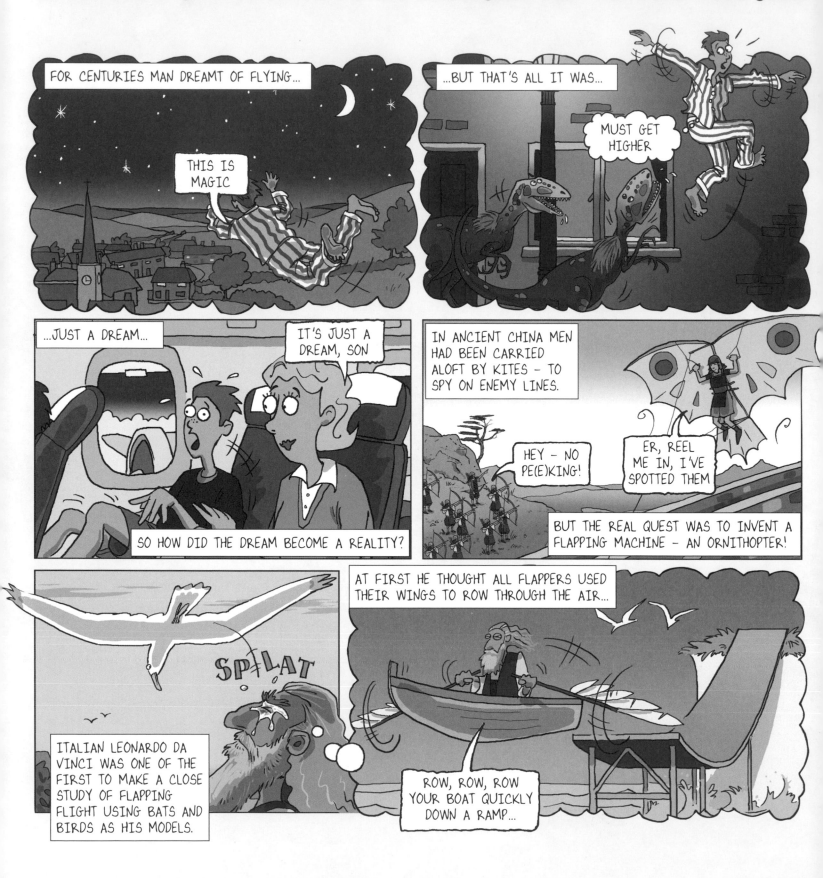

FOR CENTURIES MAN DREAMT OF FLYING...

THIS IS MAGIC

...BUT THAT'S ALL IT WAS...

MUST GET HIGHER

...JUST A DREAM...

IT'S JUST A DREAM, SON

SO HOW DID THE DREAM BECOME A REALITY?

IN ANCIENT CHINA MEN HAD BEEN CARRIED ALOFT BY KITES – TO SPY ON ENEMY LINES.

HEY – NO PE(E)KING!

ER, REEL ME IN, I'VE SPOTTED THEM

BUT THE REAL QUEST WAS TO INVENT A FLAPPING MACHINE – AN ORNITHOPTER!

SPLAT

ITALIAN LEONARDO DA VINCI WAS ONE OF THE FIRST TO MAKE A CLOSE STUDY OF FLAPPING FLIGHT USING BATS AND BIRDS AS HIS MODELS.

AT FIRST HE THOUGHT ALL FLAPPERS USED THEIR WINGS TO ROW THROUGH THE AIR...

ROW, ROW, ROW YOUR BOAT QUICKLY DOWN A RAMP...

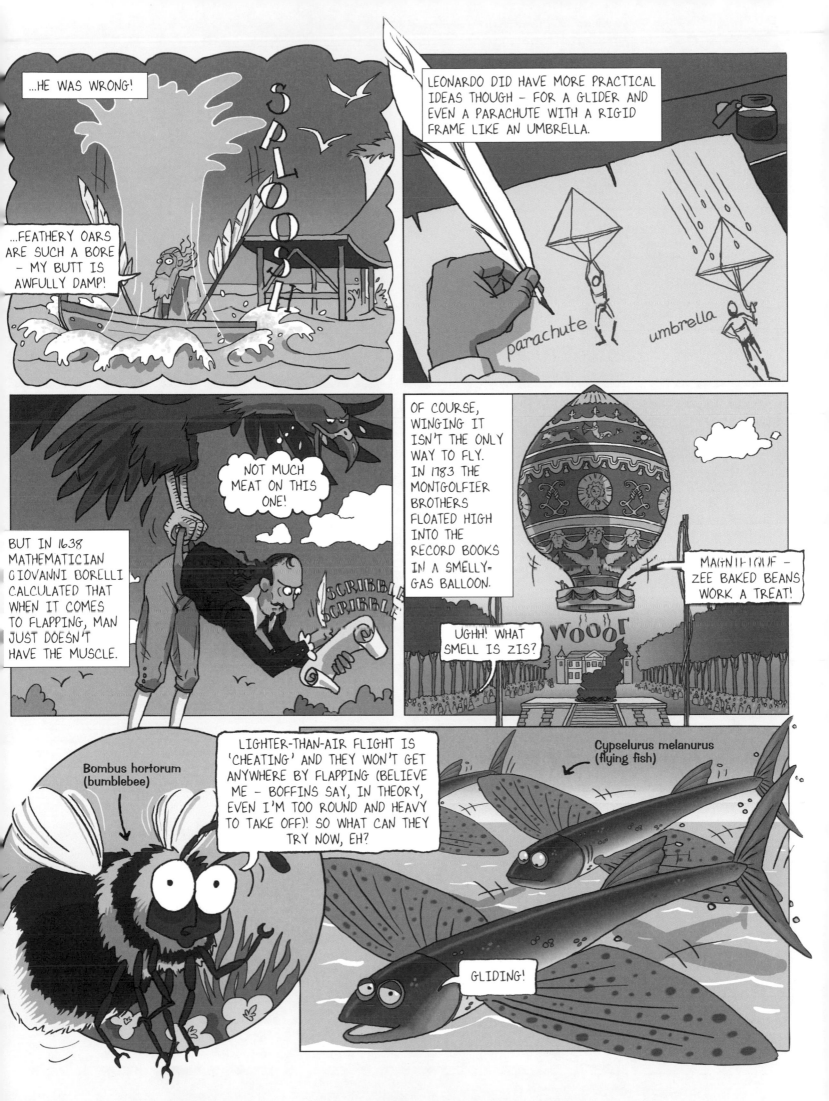

PUZZLES

DOGFIGHT DUEL

Only one of these four planes can be guided down to a safe landing on the aircraft carrier below. Give yourself 20 seconds to pick the right one. Happy landings!

Can you spot the five difference in the pictures below?

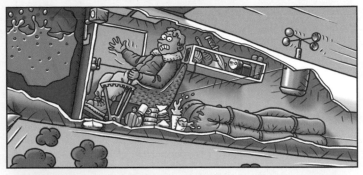

AIR SEARCH

Hidden below are 12 flighty words. Keep your feet firmly on the ground to find them.

O	R	Y	X	V	Z	E	J	P	A	M	D	N
L	R	O	S	O	N	H	T	D	O	S	A	R
W	A	I	T	A	S	R	C	N	P	A	I	E
Y	R	N	L	A	E	L	T	B	I	P	M	K
F	E	P	G	D	V	G	K	L	T	O	L	T
B	I	L	D	L	O	E	E	G	O	I	E	W
B	V	U	Y	L	E	R	L	G	I	R	R	O
E	R	I	F	A	O	Y	A	E	R	X	C	Y
U	E	I	H	N	C	U	Q	K	E	N	R	E
R	E	L	A	H	T	N	E	I	L	I	L	N
R	E	U	M	A	E	T	E	J	B	J	W	D
T	H	G	I	R	W	Z	B	W	A	Y	G	I
H	B	A	L	L	O	O	N	O	U	W	L	A

Aileron   Cayley   Lilienthal
Balloon   Daimler   Montgolfier
Blériot   Elevator   Rudder
Biplane   Langley   Wright

35

DEATH-DEFYING FLYING!

Most of the early attempts at powered flight went for an early bath, so we've enlisted our brainy boffins Professor N Large and Wanda Wye to discover the principles behind proper planes...

Let's hope you're not scared of heights, because there are lots of hair-raising heights and dizzying drops on this page.

Private eye MI Gutzache used to be a pilot, but quit for some reason. But he's agreed to get back at the controls and show us how planes work. Nice one, Gutzy!

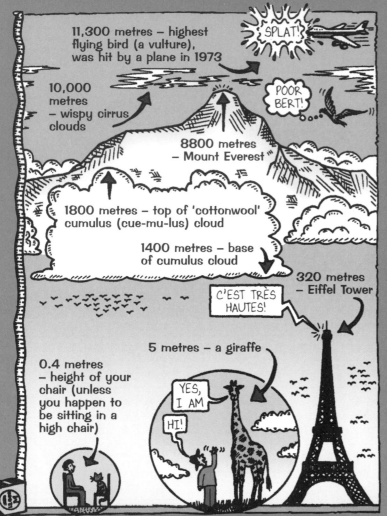

11,300 metres – highest flying bird (a vulture), was hit by a plane in 1973

SPLAT!

POOR BERT!

10,000 metres – wispy cirrus clouds

8800 metres – Mount Everest

1800 metres – top of 'cottonwool' cumulus (cue-mu-lus) cloud

1400 metres – base of cumulus cloud

320 metres – Eiffel Tower

C'EST TRÈS HAUTES!

5 metres – a giraffe

0.4 metres – height of your chair (unless you happen to be sitting in a high chair)

YES, I AM

HI!

I WONDER WHY I QUIT...

OH YEAH – I GET AIRSICK!

BLEURGH!

GROSS!

Er, sorry about Mr Gutzache's sickening problem. Here are the forces involved in flying...

thrust from the propeller pulls the plane through the air

lift from the wings raises plane in air

gravity tries to pull the plane down

air pressure presses on plane (this is the force of air pressing all its surfaces); wind also tries to blow it off course

drag slows plane down as it flies

gravity pulls Gutzache's sick down to earth

Here are Professor N Large and Wanda Wye building our aeroplane. Let's hope it won't be a big let down.

HI! WHAT D'YOU THINK?

HI-YA!

Prof N Large

Wanda Wye

Tiddles

What a drag!

You might find science lessons a bit of a drag, but drag is the force made by air hitting something hurtling through the air. It affects planes and birds… and underpants blowing off your teacher's washing line! And the faster the object flies, the harder drag tries to slow it down.

Give us a lift!

What is the mysterious 'lift' that raises the plane in the air? Well, in order to make sense of lift we need to know that air is made of countless tiny clumps of atoms called molecules. They zoom about all the time.

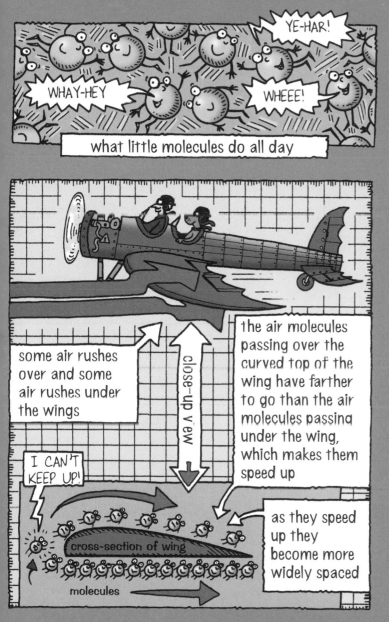

YE-HAR!

WHAY-HEY

WHEEE!

I CAN'T KEEP UP!

what little molecules do all day

some air rushes over and some air rushes under the wings

close-up view

the air molecules passing over the curved top of the wing have farther to go than the air molecules passing under the wing, which makes them speed up

as they speed up they become more widely spaced

cross-section of wing

molecules

The force of the air pressure becomes weaker above the wing than under it. Then the air pressure under the wing lifts the wing (and the plane) higher. So every plane in the world stays up with the help of tiny air molecules!

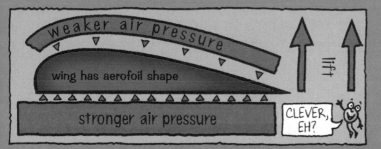

weaker air pressure

wing has aerofoil shape

lift

stronger air pressure

CLEVER, EH?

Of course, a plane can only get lift to fly if it has wings. What would happen if the wings fell off? Well, it's just what MI Gutzache and his dog Watson are about to find out…

THAT'S TORN IT!

RIP!

RIP!

Without wings, the plane loses lift and Gutzache and Watson have to leap for their lives. But luckily they're wearing parachutes. The 'chutes open and trap billions of air molecules, massively increasing the force of drag and slowing their fall. So they have a nice soft landing…

trapped molecules

OOER!

Farmer Giles' big manure heap

SPLAT!

GGGRRN!

Well, that was scientifically interesting – by the way, what ever happened to Gutzache's sick?

IS THAT SOME KIND OF SICK JOKE, GUTZACHE?

DRIP!

BET YOU NEVER KNEW!

Native Australians used boomerangs for hunting animals. The boomerang has an aerofoil shape, so it can glide through the air rapidly. The thin edge of the boomerang also came in handy for cutting open the dead animals to eat them.

FETCH!

STUPID BOY!

MAKE YOUR OWN WORLD-BEATING PLANE

This plane is designed to glide for a long time like a horrible hawk patrolling for prey. It can also be made to do tricks!

You will need:
- A4 paper
- a pen or pencil
- coloured pens
- a ruler
- scissors

folds

1 Take a sheet of A4 paper and fold over the long edge by 15mm. Fold it again and then a third time to make a rigid leading edge to the wings. Then crease and fold the sheet in half, so the folded edge is on the inside.

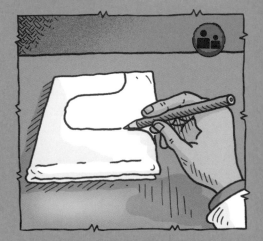

2 Draw this shape on to the folded paper. You can vary it slightly if you wish to make the wings and tail plane larger or smaller. Carefully cut out the design using scissors.

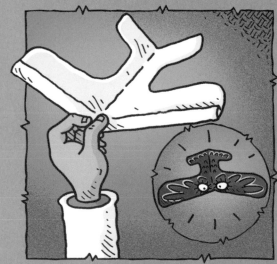

3 Your plane is now taking shape, but it needs some extra detailing. Colour the wing undersides to look like a terrible bird of prey and add big mean eyes either side of the nose.

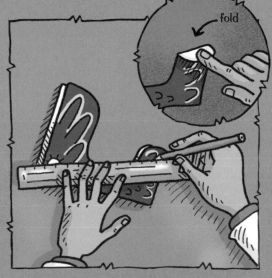

fold

4 Lay it flat again and hold a ruler at an angle so the line makes an imaginary point somewhere in front of the nose. Draw a line across the tail wings and fold the tail wings down.

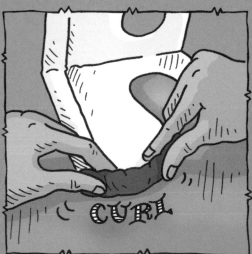

CURL

5 Using your fingers, gently curl the back edges of the main wings upwards. Curl them as smoothly and evenly on both wings as possible. Fold the outer 15mm of each wing tip upwards.

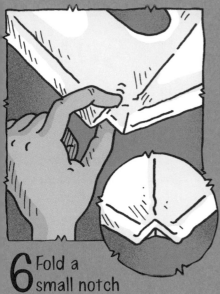

7 Time for a test flight! Find a fairly steep slope outdoors. Launch the plane by gently pulling it forwards from the front and letting go.

FLAP FLAP

GLIDE

LEAP!

6 Fold a small notch in the nose to keep the wings bent slightly upward. Look at the plane from all angles to make sure everything is balanced.

8 Your plane should glide through the air. You can make your plane bank (turn to the left or right) or even perform loop-the-loops by experimenting with slightly different amounts of bending to the edges of the wings.

FANTASTIC FLOPS

Clément Ader's steam-powered bat-winged monoplane of 1890 was said to be an objet d'art – although it looks more like a paper dart by today's standards! The self-taught French engineer's creation, named Eole, managed to hop about 50 metres but that was all. He went on to build a larger and similarly bat-like twin-screw machine, named Avion.

Horatio Phillips's multi-wing thingie (1904) certainly had some character. According to this crazy inventor, the plane hopped 152 metres – yeah, right! Mind you, old Horatio was one of the first people to realize the importance of aerofoil-shaped wings. He just made rather too many of them and his plane ended up looking like a Venetian blind!

HE'S WAVING GOODBYE, MUM!

DON'T GET TOO EXCITED

OH WELL, I'LL USE IT TO KEEP THE SUN OUT OF MY WORKSHOP!

still on the ground

SPIES IN THE SKY

Everyone likes to know what other people are up to and the world's powerful nations are no exception. In fact, as far as nosy neighbours go, they're the worst!

SPLASH!

2a

1. High above the world's trouble spots, hi-tech aircraft keep watch. One of the biggest of these is the E-3D Sentry. This controls fighters and ground-attack aircraft in places that other surveillance systems cannot reach. It's basically a modified passenger airline, packed with spying equipment and computers instead of holidaymakers.

2. The Sentry carries a 9m-wide rotating radar antenna on its back. It's so big it makes the plane tricky to handle, so no nodding off for the captain (**2a**)! The radar monitors every object in the sky in a 500km radius. It's backed up by a system which works out whether aircraft are friendly or hostile.

3. An 'interrogation' signal is sent out to each aircraft. If an aircraft replies, then it's probably friendly. No signal or a dodgy one means trouble. A team of boffins in front of banks of computers decide what to do.

4. They might direct another plane to check out the suspect. A Tornado jet roars in at up to 2.3 times the speed of sound

with an on-board camera pod (**4a**) to snoop out close-up info. It's out of there before the suspect even knows, leaving just an ear-splitting sonic boom!

5. Dangerous places on the ground – such as warzones – can be snooped on safely using a remote-controlled Unarmed Aerial Vehicle (UAV), such as this Predator.

6. Radar-imaging satellites have the most powerful 'cameras' of all. These peer through clouds and pick out amazingly fine details on the ground (**6a**). So pull your pants up, fella – you're live on a 'Big Brother' screen on the other side of the world!

7. Governments like to keep satellites secret, but amateurs still spot 'em and post their observations on the internet.

1

BOOM!

4

4a

ROAAARR!

SPIES THE LIMIT

Think spying is an ace new thing, all about hi-tech gadgets, dashing heroes and code-named cool guys? Think again! Spying is an ancient and 'orrible art, and it's been around since the first powerful person tried to find out a secret…

HELLO. THE NAME'S AGENT O'DEAR — DOUBLE-O'DEAR! I'M SPYING ON SPIES THROUGH HISTORY

THE REASON PEOPLE SPY IS TO GET 'INTELLIGENCE'…

BUT I GET INTELLIGENCE (AND FUN!) BY READING HORRIBLE SCIENCE!

NO — INTELLIGENCE IS ANOTHER WORD FOR INFORMATION ABOUT WHAT YOUR ENEMIES, RIVALS OR SUBJECTS ARE UP TO. PEOPLE HAVE SNOOPED AND SNEAKED ON EACH OTHER SINCE ANCIENT TIMES.

FIRE!

I SPY WITH MY LITTLE EYE SOMETHING BEGINNING WITH… FIRE!

YEAH, I THINK IT'S CALLED A 'HOT MEAL'

THE EARLIEST KNOWN INTELLIGENCE REPORT WAS WRITTEN 4000 YEARS AGO IN MESOPOTAMIA (MODERN-DAY IRAQ). A COMMANDER WROTE A SECRET REPORT ABOUT SOME TROUBLESOME LOCALS ON A CLAY TABLET — NOT EASY TO WRITE OR CARRY IN SECRET!

GRRR!

OI, SPY! KEEP TAKING THE TABLETS!

OVER THE CENTURIES RULERS USED SPIES IN EVER MORE SNEAKY WAYS.

CAREFUL MY FRIEND, FOR THE WALLS HAVE EARS

IT WASN'T LONG BEFORE SPYING BECAME A SCIENCE. AROUND 500BC A CHINESE WARRIOR WROTE A BOOK CALLED 'THE ART OF WAR' THAT WAS PACKED WITH TOP TIPS FOR SPIES.

TIP NUMBER 1: DON'T LET ANYONE KNOW THAT YOU'RE READING THIS BOOK… OOPS!

THE BOSSIER A RULER, THE MORE THEY NEED SPIES. THE FIRST GREAT INDIAN EMPIRE WAS HELD TOGETHER BY A NETWORK OF SECRET AGENTS AND ASSASSINS!

THAT'S CHANDRA BOND... I'M INCENSED TO KILL

THE ANCIENT ROMANS HAD SPIES ACROSS THEIR EMPIRE. THEY WOULD TRY TO GET AS NEAR TO THEIR ENEMIES (HOSTILE TRIBES, CHRISTIANS, WHOEVER) AS POSSIBLE. THIS CALLED FOR CUNNING DISGUISES!

YOU'RE NOT A CHRISTIAN, ARE YOU?

IT'S ONE THING TO DISGUISE YOURSELF, BUT YOU NEED TO DISGUISE YOUR REPORTS TOO. YOU NEED CODES, AND CODES MEAN... MATHS!

CODES
TOP SECRET

IN THE 15th CENTURY, ARAB SCHOLARS PUBLISHED A 14-VOLUME ENCYCLOPAEDIA OF MATHS AND 'CIPHERS' – CODES!

PAH! ALL MATHS IS WRITTEN IN CODE IF YOU ASK ME!

MATHS
TRIGONO
VERY HARD MATHS

IN TUDOR TIMES IN BRITAIN, QUEEN ELIZABETH I HAD SO MANY SPIES THAT A PAINTING WAS DONE OF HER WITH EARS AND EYES ALL OVER HER DRESS. IT WASN'T ACTUALLY A SNOOPING INVENTION – ALTHOUGH IT MIGHT HAVE BEEN QUITE HANDY!

I CALL IT MY SPYPOD*!

THE INVENTION OF MICROPHONES AND CAMERAS MADE SPYING MUCH EASIER. AT FIRST THESE TOOLS WERE RATHER CLUMSY, WHICH MADE SECRET RECORDING A BIT DIFFICULT...

I SAY CHAPS, WOULD YOU MIND AWFULLY IF I ASKED YOU TO SPEAK UP A LITTLE?

BUT TRANSISTOR TECHNOLOGY MEANT MICROPHONES COULD BE MADE REALLY SMALL AND SO THEY COULD BE HIDDEN EASILY.

*Of course, the Queen didn't have headphones either!

43

AND THE DEVELOPMENT OF RADIO MEANT THAT TINY MIKES – 'BUGS' – COULD TRANSMIT SOUND WITHOUT ANY SPY ACTUALLY HAVING TO BE THERE.

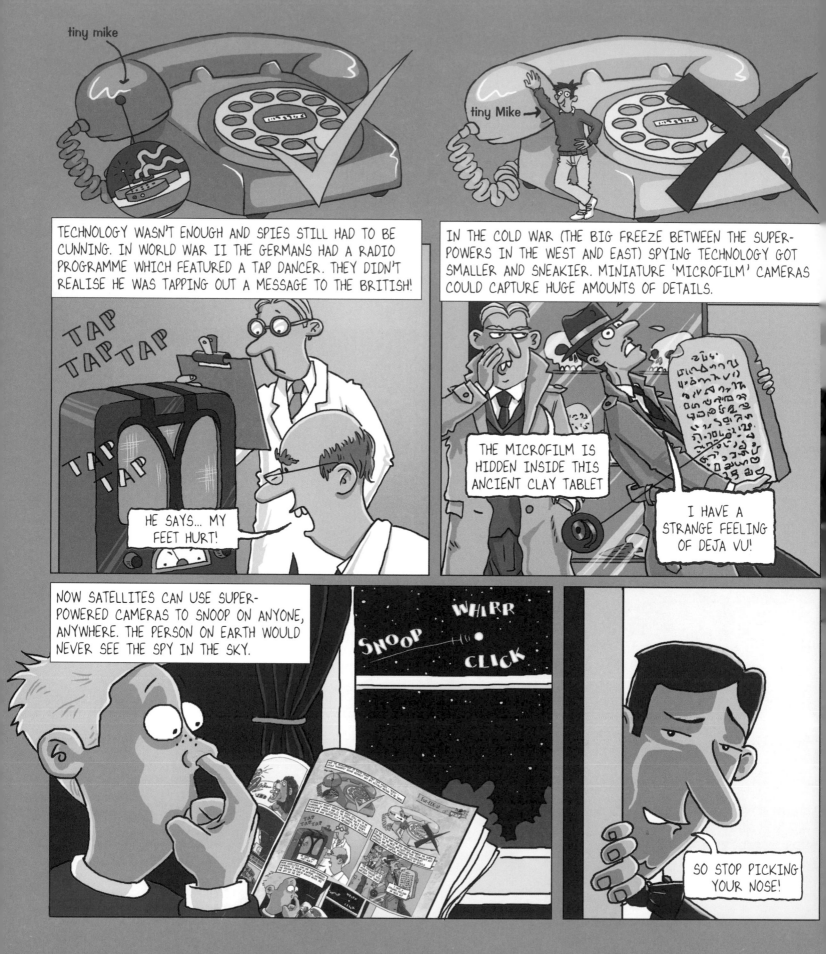

tiny mike

tiny Mike

TECHNOLOGY WASN'T ENOUGH AND SPIES STILL HAD TO BE CUNNING. IN WORLD WAR II THE GERMANS HAD A RADIO PROGRAMME WHICH FEATURED A TAP DANCER. THEY DIDN'T REALISE HE WAS TAPPING OUT A MESSAGE TO THE BRITISH!

TAP TAP TAP

TAP TAP

HE SAYS... MY FEET HURT!

IN THE COLD WAR (THE BIG FREEZE BETWEEN THE SUPER-POWERS IN THE WEST AND EAST) SPYING TECHNOLOGY GOT SMALLER AND SNEAKIER. MINIATURE 'MICROFILM' CAMERAS COULD CAPTURE HUGE AMOUNTS OF DETAILS.

THE MICROFILM IS HIDDEN INSIDE THIS ANCIENT CLAY TABLET

I HAVE A STRANGE FEELING OF DEJA VU!

NOW SATELLITES CAN USE SUPER-POWERED CAMERAS TO SNOOP ON ANYONE, ANYWHERE. THE PERSON ON EARTH WOULD NEVER SEE THE SPY IN THE SKY.

WHIRR

SNOOP

CLICK

SO STOP PICKING YOUR NOSE!

PUZZLES

DIALLING CODE

Agent Double–O'Dear has been sent a TEXT. Grown-ups find TXT talk as confusing as a code, but this person has made it doubly difficult for this dopey spy. No, it's not Welsh... it's a code! You're smarter than Double–O'Dear, aren't you? So what does his text say?

(CLUE: It's been created in two stages. First... all the vowels have been removed from the message, like they often are in a 'txt'. Then... the sender has reversed it to make it tougher to crack.)

DPTS, Y
GNHCTW R
SRDR NTCLLC
CNCS LBRRH

SPY TRIAL

Want to join the secret service? Then you have to pass this tough spy test by choosing the correct answers:

1. A mole is a spy who...
a) works underground
b) works inside an organization to spy on it
c) dresses in a black velvet coat

2. A microdot is...
a) a tiny secret message the size of a full stop.
b) a tiny spot of poison
c) a miniature microphone

3. A cam-car is...
a) a vehicle fitted with surveillance equipment
b) a camel fitted with surveillance equipment
c) a heavily camouflaged car

4. Black Ops are...
a) missions in the dark
b) bad mistakes
c) super-secret intelligence operations

5. Humint is...
a) a code written in toothpaste
b) human Intelligence
c) a chewing gum used to stick bugs in place

6. Tunnel sniffers are...
a) air sensors which detect things in tunnels
b) spies who work on the London Underground
c) dogs that spy in the Channel Tunnel between Britain and France

SUPER SPY RING

It's just a normal day on an ordinary street, but things are not as they seem! Spies are at work everywhere, using all kinds of tricky techniques!

1. These two undercover cronies are talking in a loud record shop, so no bugging device can hear what they're saying, of course!

2. Is this a sign-writer up a ladder? No! It's an agent taking top-secret photographs through an office window. Cheeky!

3. Closed-circuit television (CCTV) cameras are spying on us all the time. They are in every high street in the UK, looking out for rogues committing robberies, muggings, parking offences and other crimes.

4. This café is a whirr of spying activity. One person pretends to read a newspaper, which hides a recording device. Meanwhile, the man in a false beard (**4a**) records the conversation on a pen-microphone.

5. Upstairs in the computer room, a cunning caretaker is using a portable scanner, just the size of a ruler, to scan documents.

6. In the room above, a counter-spy is sweeping the place for bugs with his bug scanner. It looks like he's found one inside a lamp!

7. Inside the sneaky sign-writer's van there's no paint, but instead computer and recording equipment to analyse conversations.

8. This spy is trying to use his watch walkie-talkie, but pesky kids keep asking him for the time!

9. The man in the hat is doing a 'dead drop' – leaving a package in a special place for another to pick up. But it could all go rubbish if the tramp (**9a**) picks it up instead. Then again, is he really a tramp?

10. These policemen seem to have caught a spy red-handed, so special agents on a rooftop (**10a**) call off their chase. But the men on the ground are actually fellow spies in false uniforms. They've really used blank bullets and the 'injured' man has used capsules that ooze pretend blood. Now that's really sneaky!

11. Why are these men talking with their hands over their mouths? So the lip-reader on the roof (**11a**) can't see what they're saying!

12. Is this man barking mad? No, he's placing a GPS satellite device under an enemy's car so he can track where he's going.

13. Making a mobile phone call is a sticky problem, especially when your enemy (**13a**) is stopping you by using a jamming device.

DEVIOUS DEVICES

Although spies do a lot of the thinking and sneaking about, modern espionage makes use of massively sophisticated machines to monitor movement and sound. Time to get technical with some top toys.

Now you've got to grips with some sneaky spy behaviour, it's time to get tricky and technical with some top espionage toys!

Beastly bugs

If you want to know what someone is saying, then you need to listen in – which is where bugs come in handy. Bugs are hidden microphones. Why are they called bugs? Because, like a spider or a beetle, they can disappear into small places.

IT'S A BUG'S LIFE!

Hidden hearing

Bugs come in many shapes and sizes but they all relay audio signals to a receiver. Some are designed to be disguised in telephones, clocks and lampshades. One of the smallest on the market is a box just a few millimetres wide – that's tinier than a pea. If you're not careful, you could drop this bug in your lunchbox and who knows where it may end up! Other bugs look like everyday objects – such as one that resembles an electric plug.

YIKES! HE'S GOING TO EAT THAT BUG!

Dare you discover...
how to detect a bug?

Bugs transmit sounds over short and very long distances. Look at your bedroom and think of all the places a bug might be hidden! They could be:

inside a lampshade

behind curtain track

under a cabinet

behind a drawer

under the bed

under a stool

Evidence

Spy experts are eagle-eyed when looking for signs of disturbance and espionage activity. So look around for recently disturbed dust on surfaces, tiny hiding places inside drawers, under chairs or even in light fittings, but don't touch anything that could be dangerous. Found some other sneaky hiding holes? Now you're thinking like a spy!

Techno tips

Bugs may be found by sensitive metal detectors. Handheld detectors sometimes look just like a magnifying glass. An electronic bug detector – also called a bugsweeper – searches for transmissions over several radio wave channels. You 'sweep' it around the room and it beeps when you are a few centimetres away from the bug.

48

GRAB A GADGET IN THE SUPER SPY SALE!

Agent Double-O' Dear is selling some of his grooviest spy gadgets. But don't tell anyone! It's all supposed to be top secret!

NIGHT VISION GOGGLES
Very handy for night spying, these goggles amplify any tiny bit of light that's there. Photons of light energy hit a coated glass plate causing it to get 'excited' and give off electrons. These are multiplied by an extra 'channel plate' and accelerated on to a phosphor-coated plate that glows green when it is hit by an electron, making everything much brighter and more visible. How enlightening!

SPY SUNGLASSES
These must-have shades contain a miniature camera and microphone in the bridge over the nose. Pictures and sounds are recorded on a device under your arm!

A 'BIONIC EAR'
Think you're hearing things? You probably are – this loony listening bug can pick up whispers almost 100 metres away.

PEN POWER!
A very handy way to write secret messages is with an ultraviolet pen. It writes in a colour that is invisible in normal light, but if you look at it using ultraviolet light. But that's not all...

SPY RING
This fake gold ring with a tiny hidden camera was part of a Soviet spy's kit. Some new models include a mobile phone!

PEN RECORDER
This pen picks up conversations with a microphone and transmits them to a receiver in another place! It's a great gift to give to enemy spies – but make sure no one gives it to you and steals your secrets.

BOOK CAMERA
This book has a surprise ending. A secret lens is hidden inside its covers! This is very handy for spying when pretending to read on public transport or a park bench.

Telephones and taps

For decades governments have used a system called telephone tapping. No, that's not the kind that run water into your bath, but highly sophisticated systems for listening to telephone conversations of criminals and suspected spies.

HMM, THIS PHONE IS BEING TAPPED!

Telephones and taps

Modern mobile phones are easy to trace and track, even their location, because they receive their signal from the nearest base station available. They can even give out this information when switched off!

Super sat nav

Spies used to have to follow each other around, but now technology does the work! A credit card-sized black box can be placed underneath a car to track it. The box sends a radio signal to give their exact location, even to a mobile phone. This sneaky item also uses a system called GPS (stands for Global Positioning System) – the same technology used in taxis, or even your dad's car.

GREAT TRACK

IT CERTAINLY IS!

THE HISTORY OF THE FUTURE

What does the future hold? Some think it'll be horrible, some think hopeful, but it seems we can never stop trying to predict it. If one thing's for sure – it's unpredictable! We send a time-travelling cat to get his claws into it…

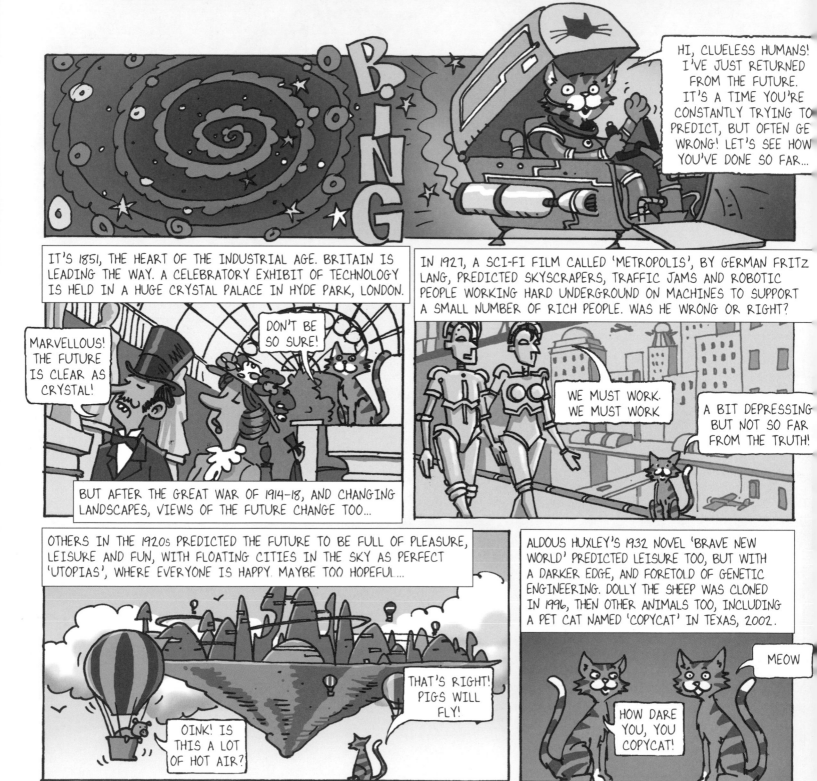

FOR CENTURIES HUMANS HAVE PREDICTED THE END OF THE WORLD. GLOBAL WARMING AND FLOODING IS A DANGER, BUT FAR LESS LIKELY, NATHANIEL SALISBURY'S 1933 BOOK 'THE MOON DOOM' SHOWED THE MOON CRASHING INTO EARTH.

THAT'S A LUNATIC PREDICTION!

SINCE THE 1930s, MANY THOUGHT THAT MAN WOULD HAVE CONQUERED SPACE BY NOW. APART FROM THE MOON LANDINGS FROM 1969, THIS IS A BIG EXAGGERATION. JACK WILLIAMSON'S 1939 BOOK 'THE FORTRESS OF UTOPIA' DEPICTED A SPACESHIP FULL OF ANIMALS ESCAPING A DISASTER-LADEN EARTH.

HEY! WE'VE FORGOTTEN A FELINE!

IT'S A REAL CAT-ASTROPHE!

BOFFINS PREDICTED THAT AT MIDNIGHT ON 1 JAN 2000, A BUG WOULD CAUSE WORLDWIDE COMPUTER HAVOC. IT DIDN'T HAPPEN!

SCIENTISTS ALSO THOUGHT SPACE TRAVEL WOULD BE COMMONPLACE. WE'D EAT SPACE PILLS AND ENERGY SNACK BARS, AND MEET ALIENS. HERE'S HOW A MARTIAN WAS PICTURED IN 1939.

enormous ears to catch sound waves

retractable eyes and nose

huge lungs

atomic weapon

disc-shaped feet with suction cups

HOPEFULLY, ALIENS WON'T DESTROY US, AS FEARED IN H.G. WELLS' BIG HIT BOOK 'WAR OF THE WORLDS' (1898)!

SOME PREDICT GENETIC ENGINEERING WILL ALLOW HUMANS TO LIVE FOR EVER. BUT UNTIL THAT'S PERFECTED, YOU COULD BE FREEZE-PRESERVED WHEN YOU DIE. ROBERT ETTINGER PIONEERED THE SCIENCE OF CRYONICS IN THE 1960s, FREEZING HIS DEAD MOTHER IN A LAB IN MICHIGAN, USA. BUT WILL SHE EVER BE BROUGHT BACK TO LIFE?

CAN SOMEONE TURN ON THE HEATING? IT'S DEAD FREEZING IN HERE!

SINCE H.G. WELLS WROTE 'THE TIME MACHINE' IN 1895, IT WAS HOPED TIME TRAVEL MAY ALLOW US TO LIVE IN ANY AGE. BUT FAMOUS QUANTUM PHYSICIST STEPHEN HAWKING DISPUTES IT REALLY BEING POSSIBLE.

IF SO, WE WOULD BE VISITED NOW BY PEOPLE FROM THE FUTURE. THERE'S NO EVIDENCE FOR THAT!

BUT WHO'D HAVE THOUGHT THAT CATS COULD TRAVEL THROUGH TIME? PERHAPS THAT'S PURE FICTION, BUT THEY'RE CLEVER ENOUGH TO GET HUMANS TO DO EVERYTHING FOR THEM, AFTER ALL...

WHO'S LIVING THE LIFE OF LEISURE, EH?

THERE YOU GO, DIN-DINS!

PUZZLES

Can you spot the five difference in the pictures below?

Rowdy Robot Wordsearch

Lurking in the grid below are 12 robotic words.
Can you spot them all?

L	H	U	M	O	N	G	S	L	E	W	P	S
C	T	O	L	I	P	O	T	U	A	E	E	I
N	I	T	E	P	R	E	B	Y	C	N	O	P
P	L	R	E	X	V	D	P	N	S	O	K	I
O	R	E	C	T	T	G	A	O	M	L	E	H
W	T	U	O	U	H	D	R	D	M	I	T	C
E	C	N	E	G	I	L	L	E	T	N	I	O
R	Q	U	E	U	M	T	R	A	N	J	L	R
P	N	F	G	N	P	X	R	O	C	Q	L	C
A	B	Z	W	O	L	J	O	Y	K	G	E	I
C	D	I	O	N	A	M	U	H	I	Y	T	M
K	M	H	C	A	N	A	D	F	L	I	A	I
T	O	B	R	E	T	T	A	H	C	E	S	A

Humanoid   Satellite   Circuitry
Intelligence Chatterbot   Implant
Cyberpet   Microchip   Sensor
Autopilot   Guidance   Powerpack

TAKE THAT

You claim you can put something into a humanoid robot's right hand which it cannot then take into its left hand. But surely robots can do anything! How can you baffle a robot in this way?

MONKEY PUZZLER

Zilla the robotic monkey has a tail that's four times as long as his head. His body is three-quarters the length of his tail. And his body and tail together measure 42cm. How long is Zilla's head?

RIoTOUS RoBots

Robots are the ultimate mean machines – with their powerful metal muscles and terribly cunning and clever computer chips, you'd better watch out they don't get you! It's time to fight back and kick ro-botty!

Robots are the ultra-modern Cinderellas, doing the jobs we hate. In sci-fi movies they are super-beings with scary robot-intelligence… but the truth is a little more dreary. These days robots do the dull, dirty and hard work that no one wants. They assemble cars, defuse bombs and get shot into space.

HAVE YOU MADE MY BED YET?

I'VE ONLY GOT TWO PAIRS OF HANDS!

Robots can do the same job over and over again – they can ram home a rivet with exactly the same force in exactly the same place, thousands of times a day… and they never get tired or bored. They sound like pretty dull company, but wouldn't you love them if they tidied your bedroom?

BUILD-YOUR-OWN REVOLTING ROBOT HELPER

You will need:
- nuts, bolts and other stuff for fixing parts together
- wire for joining up all the bits of electronic wizardry
- oil to get your body bits working smoothly
- a hammer --always worth giving it a whack when the delicate parts don't work

What exactly is a robot? Well, because there are so many types of robot – from industrial robots to creepy-crawly insect robots and toy terrors – it's very hard to get the bot boffins to agree. So we thought we'd ask Horrible Science hero and body builder extraordinaire, Baron Frankenstein to help. Of course, the Baron is more at home piecing together body parts, but we donated our funny bones and persuaded him to build a mechanical man instead.

scarier, the better! I might even strap some REAL body bits on to it… I want my robot helper to lend a hand with my monster-building projects, so I need to add specialised parts:
1. a funnel for pouring blood
2. a nasty sewing-needle hand and thread dispenser
3. a big, ugly syringe for injecting bodily liquids!

SUPER-STRONG MUSCLES

Robots need to get around on their own and be move their own body bits. A robot's muscles are plastic and its joints are made of metal hinges, moved by 'actuators'. These are electric motors, magnetic pumps or pistons. Unlike my monsters, my robot-helper's muscles will never tire – so I'll be able to make many more bodies… heh, heh!

A BODY

All robots need a body – what good is a pile of old electronic widgets? Lots of robot builders like a human shape because they think it looks less scary – but I think the

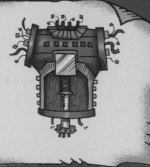

SUPER SENSES

Robots wouldn't be much cop if they couldn't sense the outside world. All robots have a system that tells them what position all their bits are in to stop them tripping up and falling over all the time. Most robots have the machine equivalents of eyes and touch sensors and some, like bomb detectors, have chemical 'noses'. It's better if my robot can't smell the putrid bits he's stitching together, but he needs ears to hear my orders!

POWER UNIT

A battery pack will be best to keep my robot up and running. (Solar power will be no use in a dungeon.)

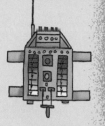

BRAINS

Not too much hopefully! But every robot needs a central system to organise all its bits, otherwise it would go haywire. These days, robot brains are all computers.

Artificial intelligence?

Robots need to know how to act in every situation otherwise they would sit around like mechanical morons. Computer brains can now be programmed to learn from their mistakes and do frighteningly complicated things, like playing chess. But does that make them intellegent? As one robot-head said...

A BRILLIANT CHESS PLAY MADE BY A MACHINE IN A HOUSE THAT IS BURNING DOWN IS NOT THE SMARTEST MOVE

SPACED-OUT BOTS

Robots get everywhere – believe it or not, they have even minced about on Mars! On NASA's Mars Explorer mission, which touched down in 2004, a man named Brian Cooper at Mission Control on Earth drove a radio-controlled rover named Opportunity about on the planet's surface! That's got to be the last word in remote-control buggy madness. Maybe you'd like one for Christmas...

FANCY A DRIVE ON MARS? ITS AN OUT-OF-THIS-WORLD EXPERIENCE!

built-in chemical test kit for rocks!

"RUMBLE!"

for just £99,999,999.99 you can own this lovely little Mars rover!

real whizzy top speed of 1.4km per hour – WOW!!!

virtual-reality kit and software to control it from your own computer!

THE SMALL PRINT
1. Mars has millions of rocks with silly names like Yogi and Scooby Doo. If you smash into a rock, you might break your toy. It takes 15 minutes for your radio signals to reach Mars, so you'd better plan where you're driving!
2. If your car falls over, you'll have to send your mum or dad to Mars to put it upright.

Rise of the machines

Robot machines that 'think' for themselves and take their own decisions make lots of people uneasy. They worry that they will soon start to take matters into their own grippers... and take over the world. But this is just science fiction – every robot has to follow a code designed to make sure that this kind of thing never happens...

I, Robot: Code of Conduct

I solemnly promise:
1. Never to hurt a human being or allow a human to be hurt.
2. To obey all the commands of my master, unless that breaks rule 1.
3. To protect myself from harm unless that breaks rules 1 or 2.

'KNEEL-Y' HUMAN!

Things we take for granted, such as kneeling down and standing up again, are stupidly tricky for machines. Trying to mimic the functions of flexible humans is horribly hard!

To do even the most basic human things accurately and reliably – like climbing stairs and avoiding obstacles – a robot needs to be stable and balanced. And if it falls over, it must be able to get up again on its own!

1. To get up off the floor, a robot must take its weight on its arms and knees, raise its hips, shift its weight through its hips to its back, straighten its legs and pull itself to an upright position, all without losing balance.

2. Movements in joints are called degrees of freedom. To move a robot's hand like a human's, the wrist needs three degrees of freedom: pitch (up-and-down) (**2a**); yaw (side-to-side) (**2b**); and roll (circular) motion (**2c**).

3. To control its movement, a robot needs a mass of control electronics. Microprocessors feature basic units. A prefetch unit (**3a**) queues instructions for processing. A bus interface (**3b**) receives instructions and data from a memory. A decode unit (**3c**) examines data and translates instructions into a format that an execution unit (**3d**) can understand and act upon.

4. Digital cameras make perfect robot eyes. They swivel so the robot doesn't need to move its head to find its way around a room full of obstacles or pick things up.

5. A robot's 'eyes' need three mosaic capture filters, in red, green and blue, to give it colour vision.

6. An accelerometer in the chest monitors lets the robot know how fast it's moving by monitoring how hot gas inside wafts around as it robot moves and tilts.

7. Balance is controlled using a laser gyroscope, like those used in aircraft and ships.
around three mirrors.

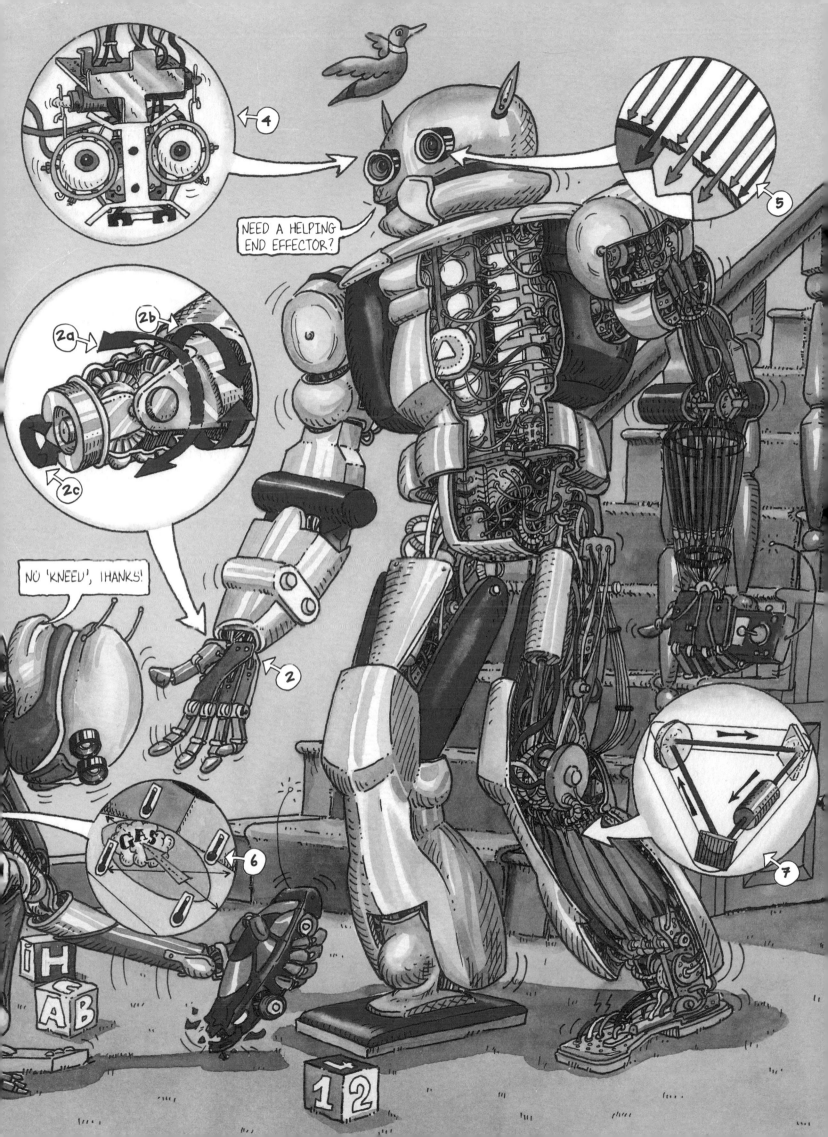

MAKE A WAGGLY ROBOTIC FINGER

A rowdy robot's fingers are bent back and forth by stringy tendons that go through the hand and wrist and are pulled by muscles in the forearm. Let's make a robotic finger to see how it waggles!

WARNING!
When you see this symbol, ask for help from an adult.

1 Trace the two templates below and enlarge them to about 20cm long.

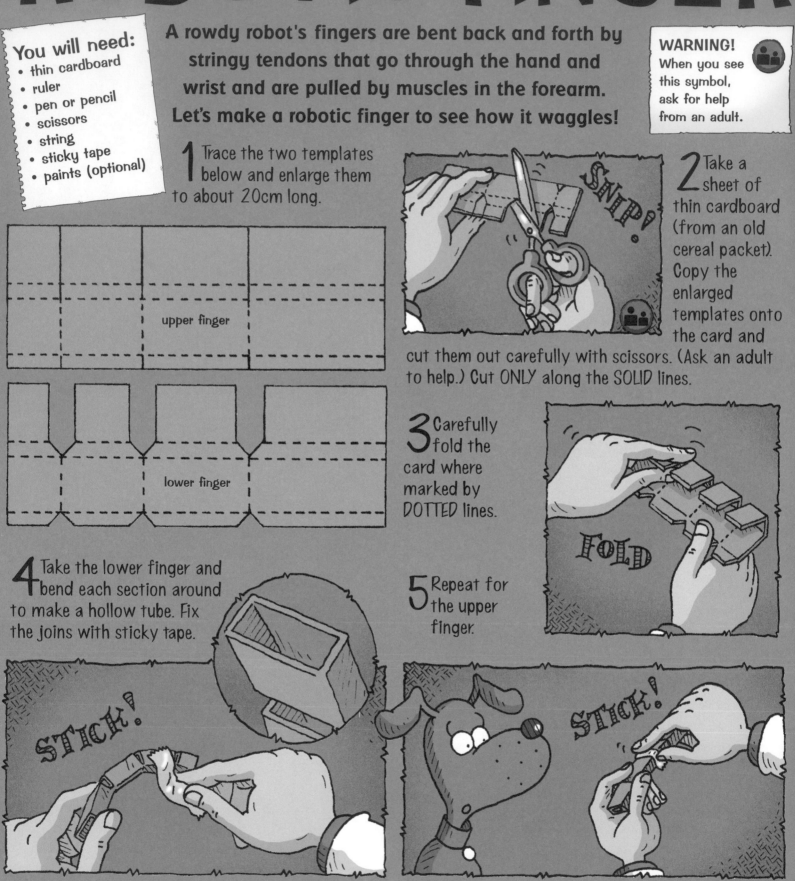

upper finger

lower finger

2 Take a sheet of thin cardboard (from an old cereal packet). Copy the enlarged templates onto the card and cut them out carefully with scissors. (Ask an adult to help.) Cut ONLY along the SOLID lines.

SNIP!

3 Carefully fold the card where marked by DOTTED lines.

FOLD

4 Take the lower finger and bend each section around to make a hollow tube. Fix the joins with sticky tape.

STICK!

5 Repeat for the upper finger.

STICK!

58

6 Cut a piece of string about 30cm long. Thread it through the lower finger and turn it over at the finger tip. Fix it to the upper side of the finger tip with sticky tape.

7 Cut a second piece of string about 30cm long and thread it through the upper finger. Fix it at the tip with tape.

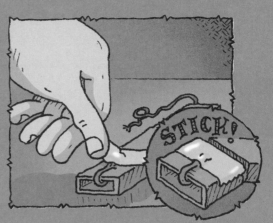

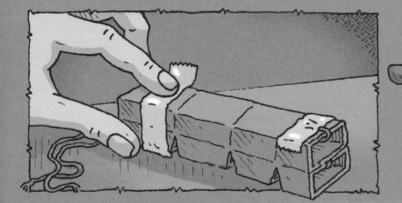

8 Fix the lower finger to the upper finger, tip to tip, using sticky tape.

9 You now have a waggly finger that will bend inwards like your own fingers, but will only bend back to a straight position. Look at the way your own fingers bend at each knuckle.

10 Now pull on the strings, one at a time. These are like the tendons in your own fingers. Pulling on the lower finger tendon bends the finger at each knuckle. Pulling on the upper finger tendon pulls the finger straight again. The fourth section of the finger is equivalent to the palm of your hand. The end of the tendon would be pulled by a muscle in the forearm. In a robot, it would be pulled by a motor.

12 To be able to pick something up, a robotic hand needs at least two, and preferably three or more fingers. And one of these must hinge in an opposite direction (like your thumb). Try making some more fingers and attaching them at the palm end with tape. Decorate the fingers with scary painted nails if you wish!

PUZZLE ANSWERS

Are you a brilliant boffin or brain-dead buffoon? Find out how you rated with the Horrible Science annual's beastly, boggling brainteasers…

Spit It Out (p.17)

Pianos, toilets, hats and sandwiches do not come out of volcanoes. But all the other things do. Here are some explanations:

- Bomb: this is a piece of melted rock, which the volcano spits out.
- Breadcrust: a breadcrust bomb is a volcanic bomb which has a cracked surface, making it look a bit like a loaf of crusty bread! Not great for sandwiches though!
- Rope: this is a type of lava that cools to look like bits of twisted rope.
- Fish: when Mt Tungurahua in Ecuador erupted in 1886, the volcano spat out fish! Apparently the fish were living in a lake in the crater.
- Pillow: a type of lava formed underwater which cools to look like – yep you've guessed it – pillows.
- Ash: of course ash comes out of a volcano, but it's not quite the same as normal ash! Volcanic ash is made up of tiny bits of rock.
- Pumice stone: they may end up in your bath tub, but they start off in a volcano. Pumice is the only rock that floats. This is because bubbles of gas in the lava get trapped as it cools.

- Curtains: a curtain of fire is when lots of fountains of lava all merge together in a row.
- Hair: Pele's hair is the name for fine, glassy strands of lava. (Pele is the Hawaiian goddess of fire!)

Wicked Wordsearch (p.17)

S	R	C	Y	C	K	F	D	P	R	T	S	O
P	U	U	R	C	I	D	O	T	P	I	L	D
O	A	K	K	E	L	O	R	S	S	F	L	I
T	S	E	O	O	T	I	Z	Y	S	N	X	P
A	O	R	G	N	A	A	H	O	W	I	L	L
R	N	A	K	S	A	P	C	Q	S	W	L	O
E	I	K	S	P	O	H	T	E	E	E	C	D
C	D	I	U	L	L	S	Y	E	Q	W	M	O
I	C	Z	E	C	I	S	S	A	R	U	J	C
R	M	O	P	A	N	G	A	E	A	U	S	U
T	C	M	P	Y	W	P	I	W	N	I	D	S
S	F	T	Y	R	A	N	N	O	S	A	U	R
Q	C	Y	J	G	I	I	I	B	T	Q	U	Y

Spot the Difference (p.17)

60

Dogfight Duel (p.35)

Follow the smoky trail of biplane C to avoid a crash, smash and a splash.

Air Search (p.35)

O	R	Y	X	V	Z	E	J	P	A	M	D	N
L	R	O	S	O	N	H	T	D	O	S	A	R
W	A	I	T	A	S	R	C	N	P	A	I	E
Y	R	N	L	A	E	L	T	B	I	P	M	K
F	E	P	G	D	V	G	K	L	T	O	L	T
B	I	L	D	L	O	E	E	G	O	I	E	W
B	V	U	Y	L	E	R	L	G	I	R	R	O
E	R	I	F	A	O	Y	A	E	R	X	C	Y
U	E	I	H	N	C	U	Q	K	E	N	R	E
R	E	L	A	H	T	N	E	I	L	I	L	N
R	E	U	M	A	E	T	E	J	B	J	W	D
T	H	G	I	R	W	Z	B	W	A	Y	G	I
H	E	Y	B	A	L	L	O	O	N	W	L	A

Spot the Difference (p.35)

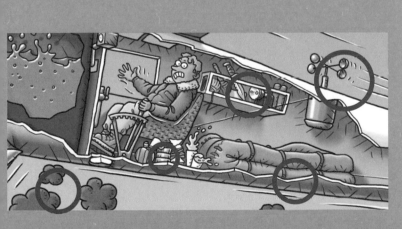

Dialling Code (p.45)

Horrible Science Collection readers are watching you, stupid!

Spy Trial (p.45)

1. b) Like real moles, these spies are hard to spot.
2. a) The only humps these worry about are speed humps! 3. a) 4. c) That's so TOTALLY TOP secret that other agents don't even know. Scary. 5. b) Humint is what your teachers don't have much of! 6. c)

Spot the Difference (p.53)

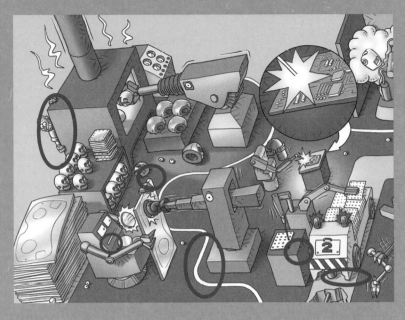

Take That (p.53)
You put the robot's left hand or wrist into its right hand.

Monkey Puzzlers (p.53)
Zilla's head is 6cm long; his body is 18cm long and his tail is 24cm.

Rowdy Robot Wordsearch (p.53)

L	H	U	M	O	N	G	S	L	E	W	P	S
C	T	O	L	I	P	O	T	U	A	E	E	I
N	I	T	E	P	R	E	B	Y	C	N	O	P
P	L	R	E	X	V	D	P	N	S	O	K	I
O	R	E	C	T	T	G	A	O	M	L	E	H
W	T	U	O	U	H	D	R	D	M	I	T	C
E	C	N	E	G	I	L	L	E	T	N	I	O
R	Q	U	E	U	M	T	R	A	N	J	L	R
P	N	F	G	N	P	X	R	O	C	Q	L	C
A	B	Z	W	O	L	J	O	Y	K	G	E	I
C	D	I	O	N	A	M	U	H	I	Y	T	M
K	M	H	C	A	N	A	D	F	L	I	A	I
T	O	B	R	E	T	T	A	H	C	E	S	A

PICTURE CREDITS

2–5 Tony de Saulles; 6–7 Yann LeGoaec; 8–10 Kevin Hopgood; 11 Geri Ford; 11–12 Tom Connell; 14–15 Paul Peart–Smith; 16 Gemma Hastilow; 17(tr) Kevin Hopgood, (l) Tom Connell; 18–19 Dave Smith; 20–22 Kevin Hopgood; 23 Tony de Saulles; 24–25 Tom Connell; 26 Gemma Hastilow; 27 Tony de Saulles; 28–29 Robin Carter; 30–31 Dave Smith; 32–34 Geri Ford; 35(tr) Tom Connell, (l) Gary Northfield; 36–37 Tony de Saulles; 38 Gemma Hastilow; 39 Tony de Saulles; 40–41 Yann LeGoaec; 42–44 Geri Ford; 45 Gary Northfield; 46–47 Patrice Aggs; 48–49 Paul Peart–Smith; 50–52 Rob Davies; 53(tr) Tom Connell, (cr) Gary Northfield; 54–55 Gary North-field; 55(cr) Tony de Saulles; 56–57 Yann LeGoaec; 58–59 Gemma Hastilow; 60 Kevin Hopgood; 61 Tom Connell; 62–63 Tony de Saulles